Airplane with History

Cessna A-37B Dragonfly 605

Julio Arróspide Rivera

Aviation Art & History

Airplane with History: Cessna A-37B Dragonfly 605

First Edition, August 2022.

Legal Representative: **Julio Arróspide Rivera**
ISBN: **9798847069687**
Graphic Design: **Julio Arróspide Rivera**
Mail: julio.arrospide@aviationarthistory.com
Printed by Amazon KDP

All rights reserved, prohibited the total or partial reproduction of this book in any means of distribution without prior permission of its authors.

COPYRIGHT information

NOTICE

"No effort was spared to trace down the original owners/authors of the pictures in this book in order to give them full credit and to obtain authorization for publication. This, however, in some cases turned out to be impossible due to the age of some of the images. If someone takes the credit that he is the rightful owner of a copyright on one or more pictures published in this book pages please contact the authors.".

Airplane with History

Cessna A-37B Dragonfly 605

Cessna A-37B No. J-605 from Aviation Group No. 1 at the beginning of its operational life in 1976, carrying four 500 pounds bombs during a tactical polygon exercise. (Vía Sergio Molina C.)

Mechanics and specialists from Aviation Group No. 1 in front of Cessna A-37B No. J-605, which evidences the change of the rudder, belonging to another aircraft, and that does not match its painting pattern. (Vía Julio Arróspide R.)

Cessna A-37B No. 605 (S/N 74-1003) from Chilean Air Force

This was one of 44 Cessna A-37B Dragonfly operated by the Chilean Air Force (FACh) between 1975 and 2009. However, this aircraft continues to operate until today, but in the Salvadoran Air Force, accumulating more than 47 years of service.

Peace Andes 1

At the beginning of the convulsed 1970s, the FACh was seeking to recover its operational capabilities to face the great advantage of the Air Forces of Argentina and Peru, product of the limitations imposed by the Military Assistance Program (PAM) by the US government.

The old F-80C/T-33A Shooting Star flew their last hours of flight and only the arrival of the Hawker Hunter came to recover the degree of readiness to face the neighborhood crises that were on the horizon, especially the signals given by the Peruvian government, which began to arm itself to the teeth with Russian weapon systems, causing an obvious regional imbalance.

In 1972 negotiations began with the United States with the new mechanism for the acquisition of weapons through the FMS, which allowed the purchase of weapons systems in a more expeditious way. The FACh requested a batch of sixteen Cessna A-37B Dragonfly attack aircraft to equip the Aviation Group No. 1, along with Cessna T-37C advanced trainers to reinforce the flight instruction in the Aviation School. This procurement was delayed by the change of government in 1973 and resumed in 1974.

(Rino Poletti Collection)

The project was called "Peace Andes 1" and the planes began to be built in 1974. That same year, pilots and specialists were sent to the United States to conduct flight instruction courses and the respective training in the maintenance of the subsystems of the new weapon system.

The Kennedy Amendment

This project was almost unsuccessful because of the implementation of the "Kennedy" Amendment, which was a measure adopted by the U.S. government to punish South American military governments for violations of human rights. Fortunately, the contracts were respected because they were signed before the amendment came into force.

Neighborhood crisis with Peru

The arrival of these planes was providential, since the Peruvians were determined to recover the territories lost in the War of the Pacific and had concentrated a large force of armored vehicles in southern Peru and their planes began to violate Chilean airspace.

Quickly, the Tactical School of the Aviation Group No. 1 began preparing fighter pilots in the new attack aircraft, which were instructed by the pilots who took the instructor course with USAF pilots with combat experience during the Vietnam War. At the same time, instructors and new pilots began to prepare war plans to confront the Peruvian Air Force and provide support to Chile's land and naval forces.

Cessna A-37B Dragonfly No. 605 from Aviation Group No. 12, during its participation in FIDA 1988, using the first version of the "Austral" painting scheme. (Via Anselmo Aguilar)

Cessna A-37B Dragonfly No. 605 from Aviation Group No. 12, taxiing at Los Cerrillos Air Base, Santiago, after an aerial formation training flight. (Rino Poletti B. Collection)

(Andrés Contador K.)

...essna A-37B No. 605 on the flight line of Aviation Group No. 3, which was ...activated at the Maquehue Air Base in Temuco, waiting for the arrival of ten ...essna OA-37B acquired from the United States in 1992. (Rino Poletti B. Collection)

...essna A-37B No. 605 during a static presentation at Chabunco Air Base, Punta ...enas. It shows the arsenal of tactical charges that the aircraft could employ. (Via ...io Arróspide R.)

Transfer to Aviation Group No. 12

Cessna A-37B No. J-605 faces the crisis of 1978 deployed in different redeployment airfields in the Chilean North with the mission of attacking Peruvian and Argentine targets. After the crisis, the plane received a change in its painting scheme, with lighter tones and a new pattern of spots, decreasing the size of the numerals and the application of stencils in Spanish. In 1981 its registration was simplified, removing the prefix "J", remaining as No. 605.

In mid-1982 it was transferred to Aviation Group No. 12 and from 1984 it began to sport the first version of the "Austral" painting scheme, with a medium green color base with dark green spots and a large numeral format in white color.

In 1992 it was commissioned to the Aviation Group No. 3 at the Maquehue Air Base in Temuco, for training the crews that would transfer in flight ten OA-37B aircraft acquired to the United States. Once the new fleet was operational, 605 was returned to Aviation Group No. 12.

In 1996, the A-37B fleet was the first to employ its self-transfer capability through In-Flight Refueling operations.

Exercise Crucex III

Cessna 605 was part of the six FACh's A-37B from Aviation Group No. 12 that self-transferred to Annapolis, Brazil, to participate in the multinational Exercise Crucex III, in August 2006.

3 (Ricardo Alas)

Ending of its operational life in Chile

Cessna No. 605 ended its operational life in December 2009 in a farewell ceremony attended by representatives of the generations of fighter pilots who were trained in the Dragonfly.

A number of aircraft were donated to be a source of instruction for the students from the School of Specialties, others were placed as monuments, but most were preserved in the Supply Wing waiting for their destination. Finally, some were sold to the AMARG regeneration center, others to the air forces of Uruguay and Colombia and ten aircraft were sold in 2014 to the Salvadoran Air Force (FAS), including No. 605.

New home for No. 605

At present, the Cessna A-37B S/N 74-1003 continues to serve in the FAS, identified as FAS 442 and is part of the Fighter and Bombardment Group of the Second Air Brigade, along with the rest of the A-37 of the FAS. The aircraft retained the scheme of the upper surfaces used in the FACh and with its lower surfaces in a light grey color with wavy finials. It also sports on its lower surface the figure of a dragon painted in black.

Cessna FAS 440 made a flight presentation along with FAS 440, during the celebration of the Centenary celebration of the Guatemalan Air Force, at La Aurora airport, on December 5, 2021, presenting himself as the "Cuscatlán" Squadron.

Cessna A-37B Dragonfly No. 605 from Aviation Group No. 12, parked on the Aviation Group No. 10 flight line, during its participation in FIDAE 2008. (André Contador K.)

Cessna A-37B Dragonfly FAS 442 of the Salvadoran Air Force, ex FACh No. 605. The aircraft retained part of the Chilean painting scheme and a light gray tone was applied to the lower surfaces with a wavy finish. (Ricardo Fernández)

Service Log

Date	Organization	Model	Register	Notes
00-00-1974	Cessna	A-37B	74-1003	Manufacturing.
00-00-1975	Cessna	A-37B	J-605	Delivered to the Chilean Air Force.
00-00-1975	FACh	A-37B	J-605	It is assigned to the Tactical School of the Aviation Group No. 1.
00-12-1978	FACh	A-37B	J-605	It participates in the Beagle Crisis.
00-00-1980	FACh	A-37B	J-605	Change of desert painting scheme.
00-10-1981	FACh	A-37B	605	Register is modified, eliminating the prefix "J".
00-06-1982	FACh	A-37B	605	It is transferred to the Aviation Group No. 12, Chabunco Air Base, Punta Arenas.
00-00-1984	FACh	A-37B	605	Received the first version of the "Austral" painting scheme.
00-03-1992	FACh	A-37B	605	It is transferred to the Aviation Group No. 3, Maquehue Air Base, Temuco.
00-00-1996	FACh	A-37B	605	The in-flight refueling system is enabled.
00-08-2006	FACh	A-37B	605	Participated in the Exercise Cruzex III in Anápolis, Brazil.
00-03-2009	FACh	A-37B	605	Participated in the 79th Anniversary of the FACh at El Tepual Air Base, Puerto Montt.
00-12-2009	FACh	A-37B	605	It is withdrawn from service.
00-00-2010	FACh	A-37B	605	It is transferred to Santiago and stored in the Supply Wing.
00-00-2014	FACh	A-37B	442	It is sold to the Salvadoran Air Force.
00-00-2014	FAS	A-37B	442	He is assigned to the Fighter and Bombardment Group of the Second Air Brigade of the FAS.
05-12-2021	FAS	A-37B	442	Participated in the 100th Anniversary of the Guatemalan Air Force.

5   (Rino Poletti B. Collection)

6   (Christian Figueroa)

7   (Andrés Contador K.)

9 (Esteban Gabriel Brea)

10 (Andrés Contador K.)

11 (Andrés Contador K.)

12 (Via Dan Toro A.)

13 (Adrián Urréjola)

14 (José David Reyes)

Detail of Photographs

1 Rare color photograph of the Cessna A-37B Dragonfly No. J-605, belonging to the Aviation Group No. 1, undergoing inspection by specialists in the late 1970s. The aircraft sports a variation of the original painting scheme that changed the tonality colors, size of numerals, Spanish stenciling, and stain patterns. (Rino Poletti B. Collection)

3 Interesting photograph of the Cessna A-37B Dragonfly No. 442 (Ex FACh No. 605) of the Salvadoran Air Force showing the lower surfaces in flight and the particular application of a black painted dragon that some aircraft have sported for a while. The aircraft carries four auxiliary fuel tanks. The ex-Chilean Dragonfly kept the "Austral" painting scheme. (Ricardo Alas)

5 Cessna A-37B No. 605 from Aviation Group No. 12 parked on the flight line of the Aviation Group No. 3, at the Maquehue Air Base, Temuco. This aircraft, along with four more aircraft, were commissioned to the Aviation Group No. 3 in 1992 for training the crews that carried out the transfer of ten Cessna A-37B acquired from the United States National Guard. (Rino Poletti B. Collection)

7 Cessna A-37B Dragonfly No. 605 from Aviation Group No. 12, landing at the Arturo Merino Benítez Airport on November 3, 2006, after participating in the aerial deployment on the occasion of the change of the Commander in Chief of the Chilean Air Force. The plane carries six auxiliary fuel tanks for the transfer from its main base in Punta Arenas. (Andrés Contador K.)

9 Cessna A37B Dragonfly No. 605 from Aviation Group No. 12, taxiing towards the flight line of Aviation Group No. 10 at the Pudahuel Air Base, Santiago, after making an aerial presentation during FIDAE 2008, on April 5. The plane configured with only two auxiliary fuel tanks to perform its presentations and improve its performance in flight. (Esteban Gabriel Brea)

11 Cessna A-37B Dragonfly No. 605 from Aviation Group No. 12, photographed on the flight line of the Aviation Group No. 10 at the Pudahuel Air Base, during its participation in FIDAE 2008, on April 2. The aircraft is configured with one auxiliary fuel tank per wing to improve its performance in aerial presentations. Sports the latest version of the "Austral" painting scheme. (Andrés Contador K.)

13 Cessna A-37B Dragonfly No. 442 from the Salvadoran Air Force (Ex FACh No. 605), flying in formation with No. 440 as part of the "Cuscatlán" Squadron, during an aerial presentation in La Aurora, Guatemala, on December 5, 2021, during the celebration of 100 years of the Guatemalan Air Force. For their introduction they were configured without auxiliary fuel tanks. (Andrián Urréjola)

2 Cessna A-37B Dragonfly No. 605 from Aviation Group No. 12, photographed on the flight line of the Aviation Group No. 10 at the Pudahuel Air Base, Santiago, during its participation in FIDAE 2008, on April 7. The plane is being moved by using a towing car (called "Mule") with a mechanic in the cockpit and three assistants to check the clearances during parking. (Andrés Contador K.)

4 Front view of the Cessna A-37B Dragonfly No. 605, belonging to the Aviation Group No. 12, during its participation in FIDAE 2008, on March 31. You can see the protection grids of the engine air intake nozzles in the extended position. During the operation on the ground these devices protect the engines from the ingestion of foreign objects (FOD). (Raúl Zamora M.)

6 Cessna A-37B Dragonfly No. 605 from Aviation Group No. 12, taxiing at Los Cerrillos Air Base, Santiago, after a formation training practice, sporting the latest "Austral" painting scheme with the vertical stabilizer not yet painted in blue. It also sports the Austral Tiger of Aviation Group No. 12 emblem in one of its first versions and painted in white stencil. (Christian Figueroa)

8 Aerial photo of the Cessna A-37B Dragonfly No. 605 from Aviation Group No. 12. The aircraft is painted in the latest version of the Austral scheme which includes the rudder painted in blue. Numerals and the coat of arms are painted in stencil with white or light gray color on the wings, a non-standard pattern, since there is photographic evidence painted in black. (Via Julio Arróspide R.)

10 Another photograph of the Cessna A-37B Dragonfly No. 605 on the flight line of the Grupo de Aviación No. 10 at the Pudahuel Air Base, during its participation in FIDAE 2008, on April 7. The plane is being moved by using a towing car (called "Mule") with a mechanic in the cockpit and three assistants to check the clearances during parking. (Andrés Contador K.)

12 Cessna A-37B No. 605 from Aviation Group No. 12 operating at El Tepual Air Base for the celebration of the 78th Anniversary of the Chilean Air Force. This was the last displacement of the Aviation Group No. 12 before its deactivation in December 2009. The aircraft sports the latest version of the "Austral" painting scheme, with the rudder painted blue.(Vía Dan Toro A.)

14 Cessna A-37B No. 442 from the Salvadoran Air Force (Ex FACh No. 605), taxing after its official presentation before the government authorities in April 2014. The ten aircraft acquired from Chile were transported by sea disassembled in crates and upon arrival they were assembled with the assistance of specialists from the Chilean Air Force. (José David Reyes)

Painting Schemes

Federal Standard 595C

Tan 36152	Dark Green 34096	Brown 36152	Light Grey 36440

STATIC PORT
J-605

Painting Schemes

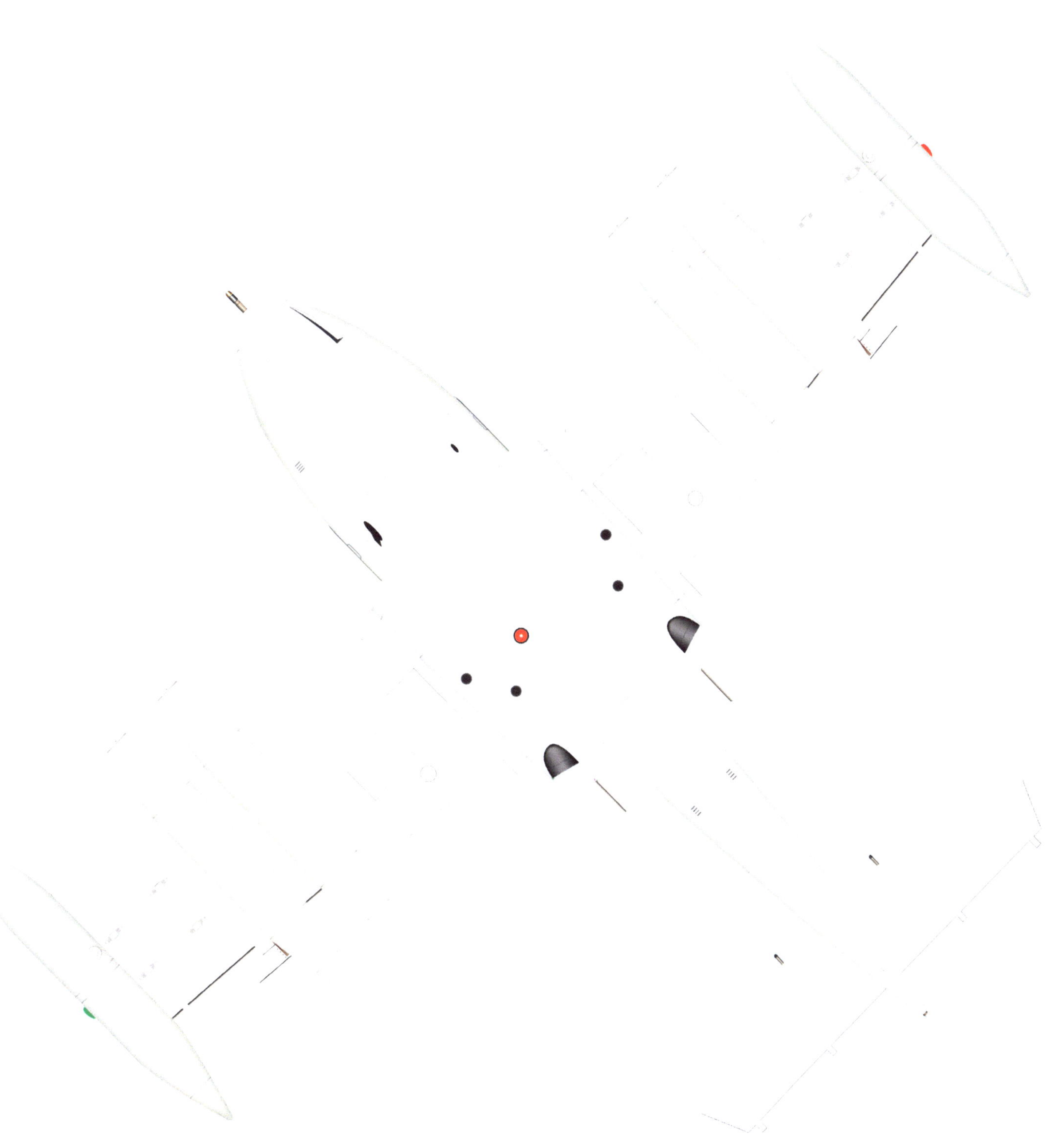

Painting Schemes

Federal Standard 595C

Tan 36152	Dark Green 34096	Brown 36152	Light Grey 36440

Federal Standard 595C

Green 34108	Black 30117	Light Grey 36440

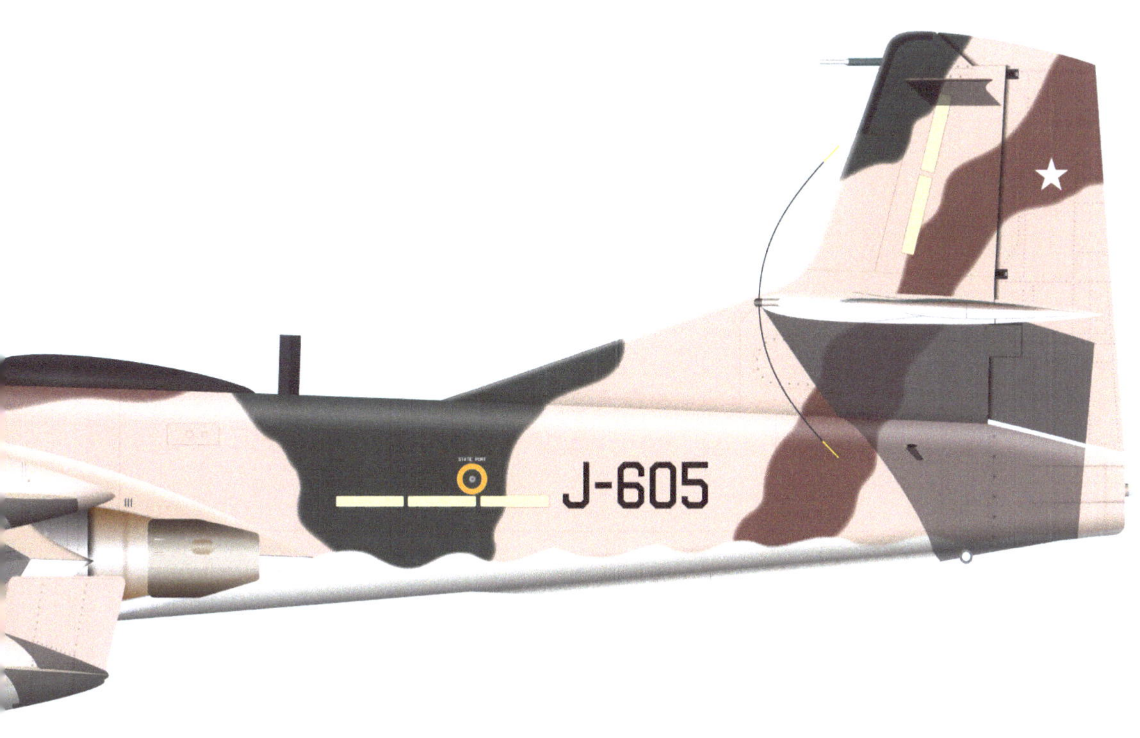

Cessna A-37B Dragonfly - Chilean Air Force

Cessna A-37B Dragonfly No. J-605, Aviation Group No. 1
Los Cóndores Air Base, Iquique, 1981

Cessna A-37B Dragonfly - Chilean Air Force

Cessna A-37B Dragonfly No. 605, Aviation Group No. 12
Chabunco Air Base, Punta Arenas, 1986

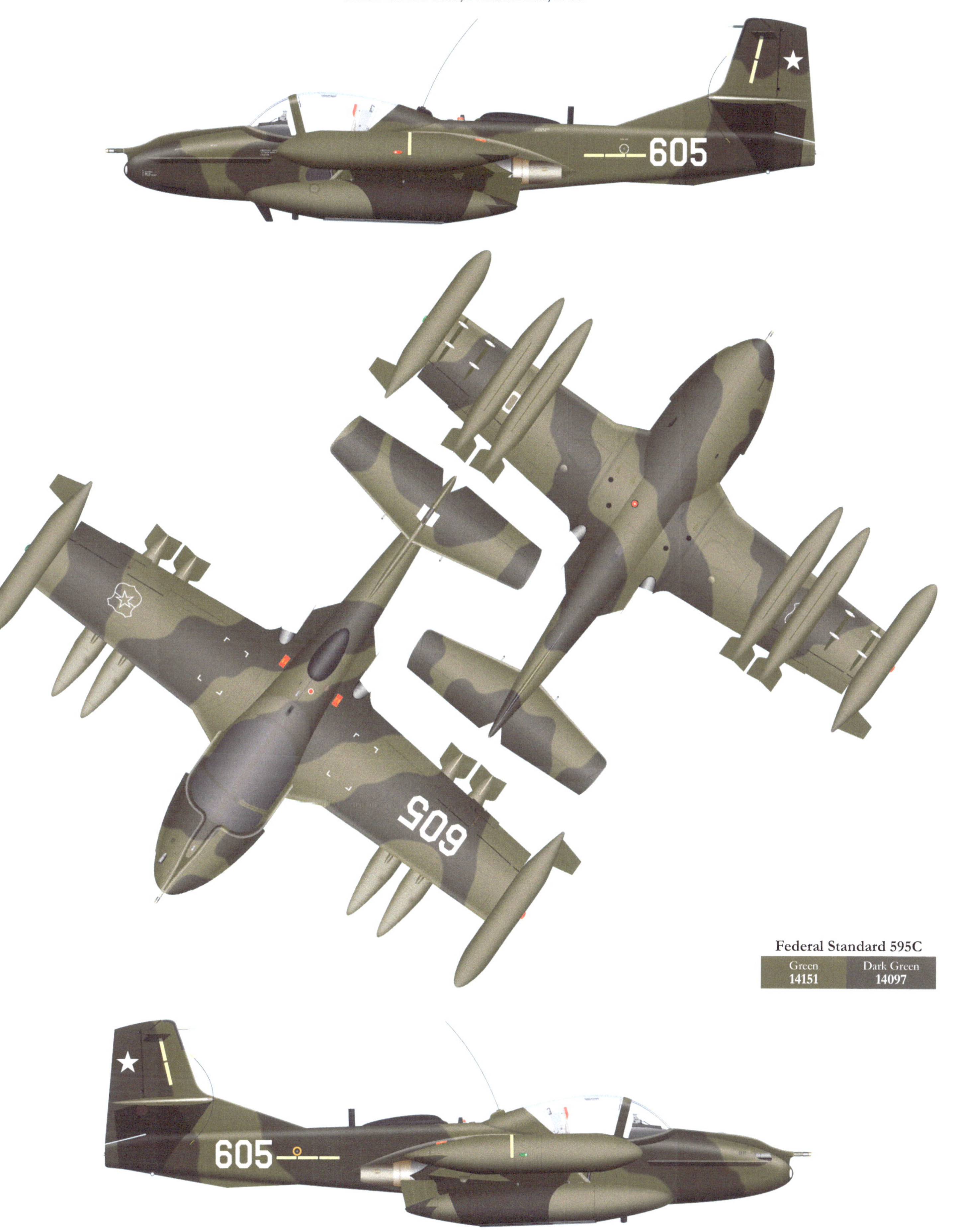

Cessna A-37B Dragonfly - Chilean Air Force

Cessna A-37B Dragonfly No. 605, Aviation Group No. 12
Chabunco Air Base, Punta Arenas, 2006

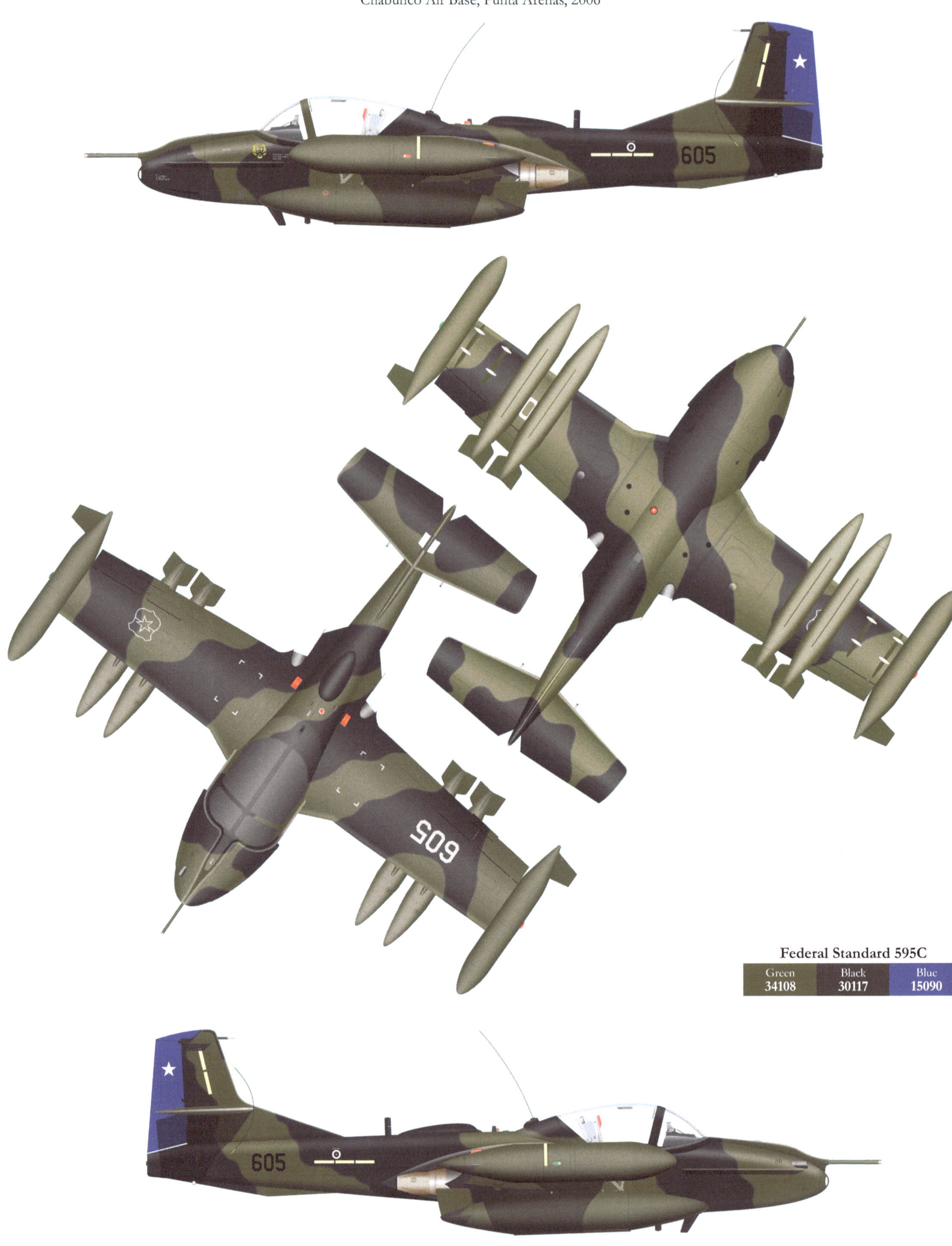

Credits and Bibliography

Credits

Edition and design: Julio Arróspide Rivera

Photographs:

- Adrián Urréjola
- Andrés Contador K.
- Anselmo Aguilar U.
- Christian Figueroa
- Dan Toro A.
- Esteban Gabriel Brea
- José David Reyes
- Julio Arróspide R.
- Raúl Zamora M.
- Ricardo Alas
- Ricardo Fernández
- Rino Poletti B.
- Sergio Molina C.

Illustrations: Julio Arróspide Rivera

Translation: Julio Arróspide R.

Bibliography

- Andrade, J. (1982). *Latin American Military Aviation.*
- Arróspide, J., Zamora, R. (2021). *Del Vampire al Viper Recargado en la Fuerza Aérea de Chile.* Santiago, Chile: Aviation Art & History
- Donald, D., Lake, J. (1996). *World Air Power Journal, Encyclopedia of World Military Aircraft, Single Volume Edition.*
- Fuerza Aérea de Chile. (2000). *Remembranzas del Grupo de Aviación No. 1, 1926-2001.* Iquique: Grupo No. 1.
- Sagaceta, R. (2008). *Tigres Australes, 40 años en Magallanes.* Punta Arenas: Autoedición.
- Siminic, I. (2021). *Rojo Uno, la Fuerza Aérea de Chile en la Crisis del Beagle de1978.* Santiago: Academia de Guerra Aérea.
- Tecnología Militar, No. 10 / 1985, ISSN 0722-2904.

Other titles

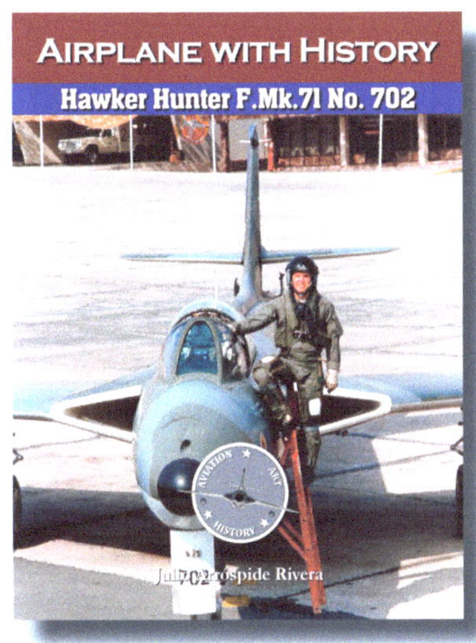

www.ingramcontent.com/pod-product-compliance
Lightning Source LLC
Chambersburg PA
CBHW042133110726
48006CB00003B/858